Jesus Christ

Yesterday - Today - Forever

ANTHONY PERCY

Foreword by
JOVINA GRAHAM

TAYLOR TRADE PUBLISHING

A Connor Court Book

Lanham • New York • Boulder • Toronto • Plymouth, UK

Published by Taylor Trade Publishing
An imprint of The Rowman & Littlefield Publishing Group, Inc.
4501 Forbes Boulevard, Suite 200, Lanham, Maryland 20706
http://www.rlpgtrade.com

Estover Road, Plymouth PL6 7PY, United Kingdom

Distributed by National Book Network

Front cover design by Ian James, JGD Graphic and Design

Drawings by Richard De Stoop

Scripture taken from the Revised Standard Version, copyright under the
Division of Christian Education of the National Council of Churches in
the United States of America.

British Library Cataloguing in Publication Information Available

Library of Congress Cataloging-in-Publication Data Available

ISBN 978-1-58979-583-9 (pbk. : alk. paper)
ISBN 978-1-58979-592-1 (electronic)

♾™ The paper used in this publication meets the minimum requirements of American
National Standard for Information Sciences—Permanence of Paper for Printed Library
Materials, ANSI/NISO Z39.48-1992.

Printed in the United States of America

Dedication:
To John Paul II ~ the instigator of World Youth Days

Contents

Foreword

The first thing that struck me when I first met Fr Percy is his frank manner. There can be no doubt of his genuine sincerity. This is true when he is engaged in important matters.

The matter at hand here is Christ and that same tone – plain-speaking and genuine – echoes through the pages of this book. But more importantly, Christ's life and heart resonates through the lines of every page.

Too often we tend to be incurious about Christ – young people especially. Whether we are well-formed young Catholics or those not quite in tune with the Church, we are subconsciously inclined to think we have heard all there is to know about Christ.

It's as though there is some finite amount of knowledge about Jesus and that because we have been so often exposed to talk of Him, we must know what he's about. I often find myself content to sit and contemplate the Christ that I know with a familiar contemplation, without any burning desire to uncover His face.

This book will cure anyone who suffers from that. It will ignite a curiosity about Christ, and show you dimensions of Him who is infinite that you had not even conceived of. Even better – the discrete, un-intimidating chapters allow you to take this journey at your own pace, without ever getting lost.

Fr Percy has always had an excellent knack for getting into the minds and hearts of young people. Here, he leads us – anyone curious about Christ – further into a place that this excellent priest clearly knows well: the fullness of Christ.

This short and dynamic book will be a perfect springboard for any person, young or old, churched or unchurched, to further their lifelong mission of delving into Christ. My greatest fear while reading this book was that at the end, there would be no more to uncover of Christ's face. My greatest realisation and joy, was that by the time I finished reading, Christ had revealed how much more of his face he has yet to reveal to me.

What will he reveal to you?

Jovina Graham

Preface

*You shall receive power when the Holy Spirit has
come upon you; and you shall be my witnesses.*

This passage of scripture, taken from the book in the Bible
called the *Acts of the Apostles (Acts 1, 8)*, was the theme for
World Youth Day 2008 in Sydney, Australia.

When Australia was first being explored it was referred
to as the *Great South Land of the Holy Spirit*. And when Pope
John Paul II came to Australia in 1986 he invoked this
evocative title once again. Pope Benedict XVI followed suit
during *WYD2008*.

The Holy Spirit is powerful. Australians in particular, but
everyone who participated in *WYD2008*, knows this to be
the case. Who could have imagined what was to take place
during those memorable days in July 2008?

WYD2008 was incredible. I called his Eminence, George
Cardinal Pell, the week after the event to congratulate him.
In his inimitable style the Cardinal said, "It wasn't a bad old
show now was it!" "Your Eminence," I responded, "it was
absolutely fantastic!"

I was the Parish Priest of Australia's first inland city –
Goulburn – at the time. In a moment of madness I decided,

along with Archbishop Mark Coleridge and the International Emmanuel Community, to hold an *International Youth Forum* for 1,800 young pilgrims as part of the *Days in the Diocese* program. It ran the week before *WYD2008*. We had our critics – let me tell you!

Nevertheless, onward soldiers march. And "march" we did. The parishioners were marvellous. Believe it or not, we billeted out 1,380 pilgrims in a city of only 24,000 people, with the rest – the under 18's – in group-accommodation. The Archdiocese was more than generous and the Emmanuel Community was simply outstanding.

But then something happened. Someone took over. We had the most extraordinary experience of Christ in the Church. It was simply inexplicable and obviously supernatural. And the same thing happened in Sydney – on a larger scale. Yes, we had done the 'John the Baptist thing' and prepared the 'way,' but then the Spirit took total control.

I was speaking to a woman of faith after the event. She was in tears explaining to me that she really didn't know the Holy Spirit. I confessed, too, that I thought I knew him, but clearly didn't.

And so I felt moved to "give something back." This book is a simple book designed to help people – especially young people – encounter and experience Jesus Christ.

I have read outstanding books on Jesus. Pope Benedict XVI book called, *Jesus of Nazareth*, is superb. So, too, is Frank Sheed's classic work, *To Know Christ Jesus*. Guardini's book, *The Lord*, is surely perennial. These books are classics. Mine is not. Still, I hope it makes a difference.

Paschal once said:

> *There are three kinds of people: those how have sought*
> *God and found Him – and these are reasonable and*

happy people; those who have sought God and have not yet found Him – and these are reasonable but unhappy people; and there are those who neither seek God nor find Him – and these are both unhappy and unreasonable.

Many young people sought Christ at *WYD2008* and found him. Many will continue to do so. The time is ripe. As Pope Benedict XVI said the day after he was elected to the papacy:

Pope John Paul II has left behind a Church that is more courageous, freer and more youthful.

It is time for the young to rise up and lead the Church into the 21st Century. It is my hope that this book will help many of them to be both *reasonable* and *happy*, for this is surely what the *New Evangelisation* is about.

Fr Anthony Percy
July 20, 2009
First Anniversary of World Youth Day, Sydney

Introduction

This meagre book is not novel. Nor is it a novel. Rather, this book is about experiencing and encountering Jesus Christ.

Jesus is alive. Knowing him makes a difference. Jesus lived at a certain time and certain place. But because he rose from the dead, he is to be found anytime and anywhere. So you can use this book anytime, anywhere.

Some people have never heard of Jesus. The numbers grow daily. Some people have heard of him, but don't know him. Some people know him vaguely. Some people know him well. And they love him. That's the best space to be in.

A lot of life depends on the company we keep. *Psalm 1* says as much:

> *Happy indeed is the man*
> *who follows not the counsel of the wicked;*
> *nor lingers in the way of sinners*
> *nor sits in the company of scorners...*

Keeping good company is ninety-nine per cent of the battle. Being with those who know and love Jesus helps – a lot. Those people who know and love Jesus and stick together are the *Church*. Jesus realised that we can't go it alone and so he set up the Church. The Church is Christ's body. Christ is the head. Head and body go together.

Jesus lived over two thousand years ago and he gathered around himself disciples or followers. They formed the Church and carried on the work of Jesus after he ascended to heaven. Four of those early followers wrote down what they saw Jesus do and what they heard Jesus say. Their names were Matthew, Mark, Luke and John.

These men wrote down what Jesus *said* and *did.* These four accounts of the life of Jesus are called the four Gospels. The word gospel means *good news.*

This book introduces you to Jesus Christ via the Gospel of Mark. It's meant to whet your appetite. I have selected a few scenes from Mark's Gospel – aided by some passages from the other three Gospels – and I leave you to do the rest. Some comments and observations I make might help you to reflect and pray.

Mark was a fellow worker with St. Peter. Jesus said of Peter that he was the *Rock* upon which he would build his Church. And so he did. Peter was the first pope of the Catholic Church, which has been around now for two thousand years. The Church has her ups and downs, but she stands the test of time and she is gathering momentum again – especially among young people.

St. Mark wrote down what Jesus said and did from the preaching of St. Peter. It's as simple as that. Mark heard Peter talk and preach about Jesus. Mark committed it to memory and then wrote down, in his own style, what the Holy Spirit inspired him to write. This is why we call the Gospel the Word of God.

When you read these words of Mark you come into living

contact with Jesus. You will get to know him – and if you "hang in there" – you will come to love Jesus. Your life will be different. I promise you, your life will be *very* different.

Before you read on, remember this: The Gospel is not a novel about Jesus. Novels tell stories and stories are great. The Gospel tells the story of Jesus, but in a way that no other story is told.

As you read the story as told by Mark, Jesus begins to "materialize" out of the pages. Print becomes power. Print becomes person. You begin to sense and feel the pulsating personality of Christ. He emerges from the shadows and his face becomes clear and his voice resonates in the depths of the heart.

Jesus introduces himself to you. You begin to see his face, his eyes and his body. You pick up his *style* and *way* of doing things. You begin to understand his mind, his heart and feelings. You feel his strength, compassion, love and mercy. You begin to realise the truth of those words: *Jesus Christ is the same yesterday, today and forever (Hebrews 13,8)*. Jesus lives in the past, present and future. He is alive.

Try and read this book slowly, stopping often to think about what is being said. Let the words of Christ that you see in italics sink deep within you. Stop to pray. That is, simply listen to what is being said. And then, and only then, express your thoughts and feelings to the *Crucified* and *Risen One*.

The Beginning

Jesus means the "one who saves." Christ means the "anointed one." This is why St. Mark uses the word "Gospel." The word Gospel means *good news.* The good news is that Jesus has come to save us and to anoint us. He does this because he is the Son of Man and the Son of God. For this reason St. Mark begins his gospel with these words:

> *The beginning of the gospel of Jesus Christ, the Son of God. (Mark 1,1)*

Jesus is at once both man and God. He is truly a man – he is born at a specific time and place. His mother carries him in her womb – the "space for another," to use a phrase coined by Pope John Paul II. She brings him forth into the world. He lives for a certain time and then he dies – as other men do. Jesus is truly human.

And he is truly God. Mary is both Virgin and Mother. She

conceives Jesus without the intervention of man. Rather, the Holy Spirit comes upon her and she conceives Jesus through the power of the Spirit.

Great thinkers, some of them saints, explain that Jesus is not two persons, but one. His humanity, they explain, is *assumed* into his divine person, without losing its identity or force. God takes to himself a human nature and enters time – enters our world. A human being who is God – a marvellous mystery indeed!

Jesus is like us in all things but sin. He has a human body, a human mind, a human will, and a human heart. He makes decisions; he loves; he suffers; he cries; he laughs; he has friends. At the same time, he is truly of God. He is God. He has no beginning and no end. He is from all eternity and is all-powerful.

Yes, Jesus is one person – truly human and truly divine. Jesus is unique. There has never been anyone like him before. There is no one like him now. Nor will there be anyone like him in the future.

This is the Gospel. This is the good news. We are at "the beginning" of it, as St. Mark says. We are at "the beginning" of something great. It is "the beginning" of the public life of Jesus.

It is "the beginning," too, if you stop and think about it, of our lives. Have you ever had a person like this in your life before? A person – both human and divine – who wants to be part of your life so that you can make a new beginning?

The phrase, "the beginning" has intrigued more than a few theologians over time. A theologian is someone who thinks about God. The Greek word *Theos* means God and so we could say that a theologian is a "Godologist."

These theologians have come to understand that the phrase "the beginning" has multiple meanings. It has something to do with time. It has something to do with making a fresh start. It has something to do with starting and finishing. Surprisingly, it has something to do with a person.

The obvious meaning of the phrase "the beginning" is that it indicates a specific time. When we read the very first book of the Bible, the *Book of Genesis*, we certainly get that impression. There we read:

> *In the beginning God created the heavens and the earth.*
> *(Genesis 1, 1)*

At a certain time, God created the world. This much is true. But then the context of "the beginning" is that God is starting something. When anyone begins something it creates an air of expectancy – of hope. We begin something in order to make a difference, to change the state of affairs.

And so beginning something is itself good news. Good news makes a difference. Good news changes lives. So, "the beginning" must mean, too, that the reader of St. Mark's Gospel should prepare for change – for a fresh start, for a new beginning, as we often say in common parlance.

But there is more. Events *begin* and events *end*. We *start* something in order to *finish* it. Doctors begin an operation because they want to remove a tumour. Athletes train rigorously because they want to win a gold medal. We start off on a *journey* because we want to reach our *destination*.

We begin something because we *intend* something. We are beings endowed with *reason* and we like to be reasonable – at least most of the time. God, the Supreme Being – the supreme reason – does just that. He has a purpose in mind when he begins. God *begins* so that there will be an *end*. God *starts* in order to *finish*. So "the beginning" means God has a purpose in creating the world.

What is that purpose? Theologians have also understood that this divine purpose has something to do with the definitive meaning of the phrase "the beginning." They have come to understand that "the beginning" refers to a person. In fact, it refers to Christ. The ultimate, definitive meaning of "the beginning" is Jesus. Purpose becomes *Person*. And that person is Christ - "the beginning."

In the *Gospel of John* we read:

> *In the beginning was the Word:*
> *The Word was with God*
> *And the Word was God.*
> *He was with God in the beginning.*
> *Through him all things came to be,*
> *Not one thing had its being but through him.*
>
> (John 1, 1-3)

The Word is the second person of the Blessed Trinity. God is Father, Son and Holy Spirit. With the use of our reason we can understand in some fashion that God exists. We can come to know the *Creator*, for instance, through his *creation*. We come to know the *Maker* through the things he has *made*. But to know and understand that God is Father, Son and Holy Spirit is another thing altogether. God would have to *reveal* this to us – and he has, he does.

The second person of the Trinity is called the Word. What does this mean? It means that God the Father speaks. He *expresses* himself as persons do. God is perfect. His expression is perfect. And so when God expresses himself, his expression is the Word – a Word Person.

A word can express a fact; a word can create a picture; a word can describe an event. But then a word can encourage; it can challenge; a word can change both events and people. Thus, at its deepest level a word expresses truth, which is why we dislike being deceived. At its deepest level a word expresses love, which is why we dislike hypocrisy – people saying one thing and then doing another.

The Word is the word of Love and Truth. Love is a person. Truth is a person. And that person is Jesus – the Word made flesh.

St. John says quite simply that, "*In the beginning was the Word.*" That is, "the beginning" is the Word. If we go back now to the *Book of Genesis* we can understand the full meaning of what is being said. Let's substitute the word "Christ" for "the beginning."

In Christ God created the heavens and the earth.

So God's purpose in creating the world becomes clear. He desires that all of reality would focus on Christ - would be full of Christ. All that is created is created with a view to Christ. This is so especially of human beings. We find our fullest meaning by living in Christ - by becoming Christ.

St. Paul understood this truth only too well. In his *Letter to the Romans* Paul says that "*Adam was a type of the One who was to come*" (Rom 5, 14). Adam was real, but he was at the same time a *figure* of Christ. Adam was like a *shadow* – a *prototype* of Christ. Or to use an image from the arts, Adam was the *sketch* and Christ is the *painting*. In other words, Adam finds his true identity *in* Christ.

And this is true for all of us. Since all of creation is made through the Word, – through Christ – all of creation finds its full meaning by looking to Christ. We human beings are just like *Adam*. We prefigure Christ. We are a shadow of Christ. We are prototypes of Christ. If we *put* on Christ, if we become more and more like Christ, we will understand our true identity. By becoming Christ, we put *flesh* on the *skeleton*. We put *oil* on the *canvas*. The *sketch* becomes a *painting*.

For the moment, pause and think about this: When God created you he created you as an image of his Son. You will truly become who you are if you *let* yourself become like Jesus. This is what many followers of Jesus have done: they have *let* themselves become like Jesus. They have *surrendered* themselves to Christ.

In this they have found their true human identity. We are asked to do the same. God is our Creator and thereby *states* his aim and *makes* his claim. He does it in freedom and so he likes creatures to submit willingly.

We, too, will find our full and true identity by submitting to Christ in freedom. We will become more and more human and will come to "share in the divinity of Christ, who humbled himself to share in our humanity."

Think about this when you can find some time. Think, pray and "feel" about this often. It will do you the world of good.

Prepare the Way

Mark mentions a man called John the Baptist. He was unusual – to say the least. *"John was clothed with camel's hair, and had a leather girdle around his waist, and ate locusts and wild honey" (Mark 1,6)* – not exactly normal attire or a conventional diet!

John was a prophet – a man who spoke the truth – and the land where Jesus lived had not had a prophet for many years. God was silent. Or so it seemed.

But then along came John and the people took notice. They began to expect something was up. John lived in the wilderness and then, St. Luke tells us, *"went into all the region about the Jordan, preaching a baptism of repentance for the forgiveness of sins" (Luke 3,3).*

John, according to the prophecy of Isaiah in the Old Testament, was preparing the way for Christ and he had a message that was direct and confronting. What he had to say is valid for all times, all places, and for all people. After all, John was a prophet and since prophets speak the truth they never reach a *use by date*. Before we examine his simple message let's take a look at what *preparation* means in the Bible.

Preparation in the Bible means what we normally understand it to mean. We prepare food for a meal, a party, a gathering. We prepare our day by looking at our diaries. We prepare ourselves to make speeches. We prepare to make a journey. In fact, most of life can be seen as a "preparation." We are continually preparing for things, for events, for encounters with people, etc.

Life is not a lottery. Rather, success or failure hinges on preparation. Preparation leads to performance. The better we prepare, the better the performance. Of course, nothing is one hundred per cent guaranteed. Things can – and do – go wrong, despite our best efforts. But normally things go well if we prepare in advance. As coaches of elite athletes tell us, the more a sportsman practises – the luckier he gets!

The Bible is no different. We see there that God prepares things, just as we do. However, the Bible adds an extra dimension that is rather fascinating. It's this: in the Bible preparation is *prefigurement*.

This means that when God prepares for an event, he puts in play another event that is mysteriously like the one he is preparing for. So not only does he prepare for events with events, but the events that do the preparing are very much like the event that is being prepared.

For instance, in the Old Testament in the *Book of Genesis* – chapter 22 – Abraham is asked to sacrifice his son Isaac as a test of his faith and obedience. Abraham obeys. But just before carrying out this extremely painful act God intervenes and provides a ram to be sacrificed in place of Isaac. Abraham's faith was tested and he was not found wanting.

But this event, real as it is, is also a prefiguring of the

sacrifice of Jesus Christ. God the Father – not Abraham – delivers his Son, Jesus Christ – not Isaac – into evil men who kill Jesus by nailing him to a cross. The sacrifice of Jesus Christ on the Cross was prefigured by the sacrifice of Isaac.

Again, in the *Book of Genesis* – chapter 14 – we find a man called Melchizedek. He comes with an offering of bread and wine. No ones seemed to know where he came from or where he went. He appeared to have no beginning or end. In this he is prefiguring Jesus who has no beginning or end and who offered bread and wine at the Last Supper and turned these basic elements into his body and blood.

God prepares us for the mystery of Christ and the gift of Christ's body and blood with the figure of Melchizedek in the Old Testament. In this we can see that God takes great care in his work of preparation. He prepares in a way that lets us see – in some mysterious way – what he is in fact going to do.

For God, therefore, preparation is prefigurement. The Bible is full of these prefiguring events. Many of the Old Testament realities point us firmly in the direction of New Testament realities. And naturally enough, as we discover this truth, not only are we amazed, but also our faith is strengthened. God's preparation is magnificent and magnanimous. We begin to understand how God goes about his business.

All of this is true of John the Baptist, who incidentally was prefigured by another Old Testament prophet called Elijah. John was sent by God to prepare the way of Jesus. He did this not only with his words, but also with his life. It was, in fact, his rigorous way of living that caught the people's attention.

John said two things that will help you in preparing to meet Jesus. First, he said: "*repent.*" St. Mark tells us that "*John the Baptiser appeared in the wilderness, preaching a baptism of repentance for the forgiveness of sins"* (Mark 1,4).

In the Bible, this repentance means to "turn around" and walk in the opposite direction. One of the meanings of sin in the Bible is to "miss the mark." Imagine a plane scheduled to leave Australia for India. Instead of flying north, it flies to the Antarctica! The plane needs to turn around and find its true flight path.

To repent means to "walk" a "path" that you have not been walking. It means to come out of the "darkness" into the "light." In other words, it means: clean up your life – get your act together. Acknowledge your failures, your sins and infidelities. That is, be honest. Call a spade a spade. Don't kid yourself. Admit honestly – gently – that you have done wrong. Admit that in areas of your life – perhaps more than a few – you have "lost the plot."

Now here is the interesting thing: John also insisted that God does not expect this *repentance* to come only from you. No, God himself will help you to repent and furthermore, he will see to it that you go about repenting in the right manner. John promised that the Holy Spirit would baptise people and so prepare them to know and love Jesus.

St. Mark puts it this way:

> *And John preached, saying, "After me comes he who is mightier than I, the thong of whose sandals I am not worthy to stoop down and untie. I have baptised you with water, but he will baptise you with the Holy Spirit."* (Mark 1,7-9)

Change is difficult. But when we realise that we ourselves can rely on the Holy Spirit – that Spirit of Power – to help us effect change in our lives, then a deep sense of trust and peace enters our being.

And besides, the kind of change that is asked of us is not all that unusual. While John the Baptist himself dressed in a peculiar manner, had strange eating habits and lived in the wilderness, this is not what is asked of us. John was a prophet and he wanted us to take notice. He was after all, the very last prophet to prepare the way for Christ. His manner of life had to catch our attention.

His message of repentance, however, has a tone of normalcy about it. St. Luke expands on St. Mark's account of John's message. The crowds of people listened to John and were intrigued with his approach and so they ask him, *"What then shall we do?"*

St. Luke continues:

> *John answered them, "He who has two coats, let him share with him who has none; and he who has food, let him do likewise." Tax collectors also came to be baptised, and said to him, "Teacher, what shall we do?" And he said to them, "Collect no more than is appointed you." Soldiers also asked him, "And we, what shall we do?" And he said to them, "Rob no one by violence or by false accusation, and be content with your wages."* (Luke 3, 10-14)

Repentance is "movement." It is movement of the heart. It is a move away from self to others and to God. Hence John the Baptist encourages us to share our cloaks – our material possessions – with others. We are called to "see" their needs first. We are encouraged to be just in our dealings with others. And so, tax collectors – those who hold the "purse strings" – need to be honest. Soldiers need to be truthful in speech and grateful for what they receive. Soldiers need to "fight" clean. And since life is a struggle and a battle at times, we all need to be good "soldiers" by way of truthfulness and gratitude.

In other words, repentance means *we should do what we are supposed to do*. The call to repentance is not a call to abandon what we normally do, but to do what we normally do with a new spirit of generosity, justice, truthfulness and gratitude. In this way, we prepare the way of the Lord. We make ready for Christ's entry into our lives.

Pause now for a few moments or perhaps for a longer period. Feel free as you think this through with your heart. What needs to change in my life in order to prepare for Christ? How am I doing in the generosity stakes? Am I still stuck in a world where I am the centre of gravity? Do I give thanks for what I have received? Or is gratitude a rare movement of my heart?

Looking in the "Mirror"

We look into the mirror. Perhaps too often! What we see there is a reflection of ourselves. But now St. Mark wants to tell us that Jesus is the real "mirror."

He tells us about Jesus' baptism. The word baptise comes from a Greek word and means to "be immersed in." John the Baptist had promised that he would baptise with *water* and that Jesus would baptise with the *Holy Spirit.* Jesus would immerse people in the Holy Spirit – the life of God – and that was the key difference between the baptism of John and that of Jesus.

And that is exactly what Mark now describes. John had his sway with the people. A great feeling of expectation had arisen among them as they came before this unusual prophet, confessing and repenting of their sins and being baptised by water for the forgiveness of sins.

Now the attention is turned to Jesus. John had said that one who is mightier than he was to appear and that he was not worthy to untie the thong of his sandals. In due course, then, Jesus comes to the Jordan River to be baptised by his cousin John.

Whereas John's baptism was for the forgiveness of sin, Jesus' baptism will be that and more. Jesus' baptism is a dying and rising. It is a prefigurement of his death and resurrection and when people receive Christian baptism that is exactly what happens: they die with Jesus a death to sin and they rise with Jesus to a new resurrected life. This is the work of the Holy Spirit – something that John himself was powerless to effect.

At the age of thirty, after twenty-five years or so of working as a carpenter and "jack of all trades" in and around Nazareth, Jesus begins his public life. His very first act is to be baptised by John:

> *In those days Jesus came from Nazareth of Galilee and was baptised by John in the Jordan. And when he came up out of the water, immediately he saw the heavens opened and the Spirit descending upon him like a dove; and a voice came from heaven, "Thou art my beloved Son: with thee I am well pleased." (Mark 1, 9-11)*

Jesus was baptised and he *saw* the Spirit and he *heard* his Father. The Spirit descends upon him – he is after all the anointed one. Jesus experiences the Spirit. Not only does he see the Spirit, but it actually descends upon him. Jesus sees and he receives the Spirit. He is full of this mysterious Spirit. It enters his personal being. But then this extraordinary experience of intimacy and power is confirmed and complemented by what he hears: *You are my Son, the Beloved; my favour rests on you.*

God the Father is showering his love and affection upon his Only-Begotten Son. When it comes to love, words are not enough. Neither are actions. Love requires both deeds and words. What sort of love would it be, if the one who loved us never spoke to us – never told us that he loved us? What would we make of someone who told us time and time again that they loved us, but never showed it with constant acts of love? This would be absurd – a caricature of love.

Divine love is no different to human love. In fact, the human takes its cue from the divine. Jesus is the object of his Father's love. The Father not only speaks words of love to his Son, but he sends the Spirit so that Jesus can see this love and experience, in his human body, the love of the Father. Jesus knows that he is loved beyond measure.

As the Gospel unfolds it becomes obvious that Jesus is a man of love. Every word he speaks, everything he does, speaks of love. It is love that leads him to lay down his life for us. He dies our death. He rises to restore our life. It is all one great act of love.

And it all starts from his Father's love. And this is life. Life is about *accepting* love. Life is about *giving* love. How could it be otherwise? Life would be senseless, meaningless, just a pathetic joke, if love was not the answer to the mystery of life. Pope John Paul II expressed this profound truth in his teaching document called *Redemptor Hominis* – Latin for *Redeemer of Man*:

> *Man cannot live without love. He remains a being that is incomprehensible for himself, his life is senseless, if love is not revealed to him, if he does not encounter love, if he does not experience it and make it his own, if he does not participate intimately in it. (RH 10)*

Christ was baptised. He experienced and encountered the love of the Father through his baptism. We, too, are baptised. If not, we can desire it. The same thing happens to us. God sends his Holy Spirit upon us in the form of a dove to grant us his peace – a peace the world cannot give. And the Father speaks to us and says: "You are my son, my daughter, and I love you; my favour rests on you." Wouldn't that be something: to know and feel this love of the Father?

Jesus is the real "mirror." When we look at ourselves; when we think about ourselves; when we contemplate ourselves, we discover Christ. We discover that we are "other Christs." We have been baptised into Christ. So, we try to conform ourselves to the reality - the deepest truth of who we are.

And so in our baptism God the Father sees not so much us, as Jesus, his Son. We are "sons" in the Son. We need to look in the real "mirror" and see Christ within. This is the real truth about our lives – about our identity. When we look into the "mirror" we see the image of Christ. This is a marvellous truth, worth thinking about for the rest of our lives. It is a truth worth acting on, too. For while it is true that we are all unique, we are nevertheless one in Christ.

Imagine the difference this foundational truth could make to our world. Imagine if people started looking at each other and seeing the real truth behind the appearances. Imagine what would happen to your behaviour and mine if we really believed that we were "other Christs" and that the person standing in front of us was "Christ" too. Things would indeed be different - as they should be.

Temptation

Baptised into Christ. That is what happens and that is what we are. And since Jesus does not act alone, we are baptised into the Father and Holy Spirit too. We become temples of the Blessed Trinity and our making of the sign of the cross - "In the name of the Father, Son and Holy Spirit" - as we enter a Church or begin a prayer reminds us of this truth.

God the Father sends his Holy Spirit upon us. The Dove descends upon us and we feel the love of the Father. We hear the rich and affectionate voice of the Father tell us that we are a son or daughter of God

This is what it means to be re-born into Christ. The Holy Spirit works in a wonderful way, cleansing us of sin and granting us *new life* in Christ. We become a new creation. Life changes.

But baptism is not magic. Making that image of Christ we see in ourselves become a reality takes work. It takes effort and struggle – both for Christ and for us.

Enter temptation and testing. These can be moments of great trial and for that reason they can be moments of tremendous discovery – especially self-discovery. As a very wise person once said to me, "You don't really know who you are until you have had acid poured all over you." Acid enters the cracks of our personal being and reveals ruptures - wounds - in need of healing. Either we embrace this newly revealed reality with an increased *desire* for Christ and his healing love or we refuse and rebel and enter into the depths of *despair*.

Mark tells us that the Holy Spirit not only grants us new life, but that he also wants to test this new life – to refine and mould it. Remarkably, he says that the next thing the Holy Spirit did after Jesus' baptism was to *throw* - yes, the verb Mark uses in his Gospel is "to throw" - Jesus out into the wilderness.

> *The Spirit immediately drove him out into the wilderness. And he was in the wilderness forty days, tempted by Satan; and he was with the wild beasts; and the angels ministered to him.* (Mark 1, 12-13)

This is quite incredible. The Holy Spirit, who appeared as a peaceful and gentle dove, now literally drives or throws Jesus out into the wilderness to be tempted.

But how could this not be so? So many people – perhaps you, too – have had this experience of being thrown out in the wilderness where everything seems empty, in chaos and in darkness. Jesus, truly human, had to have this experience. And he had it to the full.

Times of darkness and difficulty are critical for human beings. We discover ourselves in a new way. We begin to understand our weaknesses, flaws and fault lines. But then we discover, with Jesus, that we are not meant to fight the battle on our own. We are meant to turn to Jesus for help. Jesus is, as Pope John Paul II once said, the *"absolute and infinite, yet sweet and gentle power"* that comes to our aid.

Satan is ever active. Jesus called him the *liar*, the *deceiver* and the *accuser*. Nothing is surer. The devil loves to deceive, to create division and he loves to put people down. The devil's work is deceit, division and discouragement.

"I am no good," is the language satan likes to hear. In fact, he inspires that type of talk. But Christ responds by sending us the *Advocate* – a word that means "one who is called to one's side." And that *Advocate* comes into direct combat with the accuser. That *Advocate* is the Holy Spirit.

Discouragement is what can happen when we attempt to follow Christ. Because of our sins, the "mirror" gets clouded. We no longer see Christ clearly and so we get discouraged and disheartened. But the *Advocate* comes to our side and turns our failures into successes. The "wound becomes a fountain," as Mark Coleridge - Archbishop of Canberra & Goulburn - likes to repeat.

Darkness is turned into light. Death becomes resurrection. Despair is transformed into hope. The *Advocate* will have his way, if we just have faith. He will re-create the world - our lives – if we permit his action to enter our broken lives.

Discouragement is the work of satan and so too is his work of division. His tactic is to get us to distance ourselves from those who are followers of Christ in the Church. Furthermore, he enjoys creating division in the Church herself. He likes to divide and conquer.

Be prepared for his game plan. Like a true terrorist he goes back to the same old hunting ground. His tactics are not new, but they are often very effective. So, be street smart. Rely on your sense of humour and ask for wisdom. You might like to stop a couple of times a day, too, and pray the *Lord's Prayer*. The very last petition focuses on our need for grace in the midst of temptation, trial and tribulation:

> **Our Father,**
> Who art in heaven,
> Hallowed be Thy Name.
> Thy Kingdom come.
> Thy Will be done, on earth as it is in Heaven.
> Give us this day our daily bread.
> And forgive us our trespasses,
> as we forgive those who trespass against us.
> And lead us not into temptation,
> but deliver us from evil. Amen.

Me, Me, Me!

Jesus returns from that forty-day experience and is full of energy. He is ready for the mission that the Father has entrusted to him. He heads north to Galilee and says:

> *The time is fulfilled, and the kingdom of God is at hand; repent, and believe in the gospel. (Mark 1, 15)*

The time has come! You are asked to make a decision. As George Cardinal Pell said at *World Youth Day 2008*, we can't "sit on the fence" – we must make a decision. Remember, Christ is alive. And he heads "north" into our hearts and minds. What will it be? Just me and my life, or will I decide to open my life to a new kind of kingdom – a new way of life?

Jesus says that this kingdom is close at hand. So close in fact that St. Augustine once said that "God is closer to us then we are to ourselves." Let's think about this for a moment.

Isn't it true that the reasons for our bouts of unhappiness, unease and agitation are because we think that the only "thing" we've got is ourselves? In fact, we are bombarded 24/7 with the message, "The only person that matters is you." Advertising thrives with this false, delusional message. It's as if people are wearing blinkers, and the only thing they can see is themselves. The only thing they can envisage is *their* plans. Everything revolves around "me." Individualism is the name of the game. Self-fulfilment is the catch cry.

Christ moves in to confront this sort of nonsense. The kingdom of God is close. That means that God is close. Indeed, he is closer to us then we are to ourselves. He is like our breathing. Christ is there so naturally that we don't even realise it.

So Jesus is stating the obvious and tells us to wake up from our slumber and recognise that God is close at hand. Thus we need to repent from an old way of life and usher in a new way of thinking.

This type of repenting leads to faith. Faith opens up a new world. We move away from a focus on self, to a focus on others and God. And thus we return to a true understanding of self. We hear Jesus say this explicitly in the Gospel. The mystery is, he says, that our life is a gift, and so how unwise it is to live life as if we had manufactured it ourselves.

> *If any man would come after me, let him deny himself and take up his cross and follow me. For whoever would save his life will lose it; and whoever loses his life for my sake and the gospel's will save it. For what does it profit a man, to gain the whole world and forfeit his life? For what can a man give in return for his life?* (Mark 8, 35-37)

St. Mark puts before us another scene, which echoes Jesus' call to repent and believe. Jesus is found to be dining with many tax collectors and sinners. St. Mark tells us that this was Jesus normal way of operating when he says, *"For there were many who followed him."* Mark continues:

> *And the scribes of the Pharisees, when they saw that he was eating with sinners and tax collectors, said to his disciples, "Why does he eat with tax collectors and sinners?" And when Jesus heard it, he said to them, "Thos who are well have no need of a physician, but those who are sick; I came not to call the righteous, but sinners." (Mark 2, 16-17)*

The Pharisees, it seems, were rigorous in keeping the Jewish law and precepts. But despite their apparent virtue they did not warm to Jesus. They were full of themselves and carried out their moral life on their own strength.

They had no need of Jesus. To be a "Pharisee" then is to be someone who *goes it alone.* "Pharisees" have no need of help; they have no faults; no weaknesses; no need of reform and repentance. They are self-enclosed entities. Everything is perfect. Their plans are without blemish. All is fine.

But the reality is quite different – as we know only too well. We are creatures. We have been created in a *state of need.* We are *wayfarers* and our journey is underway. We will need help to reach the end. We stop and ask for refuge as we journey on our way. We ask for directions. It is only natural to want to experience love and hospitality. It is only reasonable to desire help and ask for it, for the journey is long and arduous.

Furthermore, we are sinners, and so now our need is greater. We are in a mess and we need *surgery.* Jesus, the tax collectors and sinners understand the problem and that is why they have a certain affinity. They are united in their recognition of the *paralysis* of sin.

The *Book of Genesis* and St. Paul the Apostle tell us that it is because of sin that death enters the world. The connection is deep, so much so, that every time we sin we experience, in some mysterious fashion, death. Sin is a form of dying. It was this reality of sin and death that Jesus came to heal by his death and resurrection. As some of the ancient writers like to say, Jesus put death to death by his death. But the Pharisees couldn't see it. Perhaps they didn't want to see it.

The rapport between tax collectors and sinners, however, is further deepened. Christ not only recognizes their need – their sickness – but he offers hope through mercy. He looks upon them with mercy and compassion. He offers his Sacred Heart. They are sick and need a doctor. They are sinners and need redemption. They are dying and need new life through resurrection. They need the help of the *supreme, sweet* and *gentle* power of Christ. Christ approaches them and they accept his offer. Hence they dine without fear. Christ is the Lord of their table.

The opposite is true of the Pharisees. They live in a bubble of their own making, travelling through life on their own strength, never pausing to reach out for the help of a doctor who will provide healing and counsel. They live selfish, pitiful, lonely lives, pausing often to admire their own virtue – to stroke their own egos. They do not believe in Jesus, they believe only in themselves.

To repent and believe is to abandon our plans of self-fulfilment. It is to raise our gaze beyond the horizons and look to someone else for perfection. This discovery of the goodness of God, the goodness of others and the goodness of our personal existence is exactly what faith is. Faith is a *light* that clears out the clouds of unbelief. That light shines within us, pointing us to the One who lives in unapproachable light – God himself.

It is good to make acts of faith, like the father of the boy you will find in chapter 9 of Mark's Gospel. This boy was dumb and tormented. His father brought him to the disciples of Jesus, but they could not heal the boy. Jesus takes hold of the situation. He tells the father, *"All things are possible to him who believes." Immediately the father of the child cried out and said, "I believe; help my unbelief!" (Mark 9, 23-24)*

That's it. We have faith, but it's too weak. It must grow. We must say to the Lord, *"I do believe, help my unbelief."* And naturally enough God comes to the rescue. He loves rescues – makes it his business! We need then to make acts of faith in the *infinite, yet sweet and gentle power of Jesus.* And as our faith grows so too does our inner freedom. And that's precisely what we want – freedom, not slavery.

And as our faith grows, we become witnesses, without even realizing it. Others gravitate to us – we become *magnets.* St. Paul says we become the *"aroma"* of Christ. People smell Christ when they meet us.

This is how faith is spread in the world. *"Preach Christ always,"* says St. Francis of Assisi, *"and occasionally use words."* It is more our actions, our attitudes, the way we work, that spreads Christ. Words are helpful, but only if they *confirm* our deeds.

Pause and thank God for the witnesses in your life. We believe in Christ precisely because we have trusted someone who is a messenger of the good news. It may be a parent, a grandparent, perhaps a brother or sister, even a cousin, who has brought us the good news. Friends can be helpful, too. We see this in the Gospel itself where brother leads brother to Christ. The other responds based on the testimony of the other.

Ask the Lord to make you a witness to Christ. Don't try and be someone you're not – that won't work. Just be yourself and be close to Christ. That is all that is required. And then, without a lot of fuss, you will begin to "hand over" the Gospel to others. That's what we mean by the word *tradition*. It comes from the Latin and means to "hand over." By our lives we "hand over" Christ to others. Is there anything in life more worthwhile?

Fishing

Jesus centred much of his activity around the Sea of Galilee. It is a small lake, well below sea level and was the source of much activity and trade at the time of Jesus. Fish is food and people need to eat – they like to eat.

It was there that Jesus called his disciples. It was there that he boarded the boat to get away from the crowds to seek some rest. It was there that he walked on water. It was there that he calmed the sea to the amazement of his disciples. It was around this sea that he taught the people.

Mark tells us of the call of the first four disciples:

> *And passing along by the Sea of Galilee, he saw Simon*
> *and Andrew the brother of Simon casting a net in the*
> *sea; for they were fishermen. And Jesus said to them,*
> *"Follow me and I will make you fishers of men." And*
> *immediately they left their nets and followed him. And*
> *going on a little farther, he saw James the son of Zebedee*

*and John his brother, who were in their boat mending
the nets. And immediately he called them; and they left
their father Zebedee in the boat with the hired servants,
and followed him. (Mark 1, 16-20)*

Jesus sees these men and he calls them to himself. They
leave everything and follow him. They let themselves be
taken by Jesus. They surrender themselves and thus find
their true selves. So powerful is the experience that they
leave everything – their father, their fishing business – and
go after Christ.

What a beautiful scene this is! What must the look of
Christ have been like? What must the tone of his voice have
been? There is only one way to find out. Put yourself in the
scene and let Christ see you and call you.

We may be reticent to do this, because in our heart of
hearts we fear Jesus and what his call will do to our lives.
What will I lose? What lies in the future? Which friends will
go by the wayside because of my friendship with Christ?
What of my plans and talents? What of my finances?

But nothing ventured, nothing gained. Fear is perfectly
understandable, but it must be cast aside. Pope John Paul II
said it often: *"Do not be afraid. Open wide the doors for Christ."*

Fear has many sources, but it is usually the result of
misunderstanding the nature of things. Jesus tells a parable
in the Gospel of Matthew (*Matthew 25, 14-30*) that gives
us great insight into human fear. It results, says Jesus, in
misunderstanding who God is. It results in misconstruing
our relationship with Him.

The parable is about three men who have been given
talents in accord with their ability. One is given five talents,
the other two talents and one is given one talent. The master
departs for some time and then returns.

The man with five talents comes before the master with five more talents and receives the accolade, *"Well done good and faithful servant; you have been faithful over a little, I will set you over much; enter into the joy of your master."* So, too, the man with two talents. He has made two more talents and receives equal praise from the master.

However, the man who was given one talent simply hands back the talent to the master. He has not traded with his talent, nor has bothered to earn interest on it. He comes before his master empty handed. The master is not happy.

The servant gives his explanation:

> *"Master, I knew you to be a hard man, reaping where you did not sow, and gathering where you did not winnow; so I was afraid, and I went and hid your talent in the ground. Here you have what is yours."*
> *(Matthew 25, 25)*

It is as clear as crystal. The servant had somehow got it into his head that his master was a *hard man*. Someone – a parent, a teacher, a friend, or perhaps even he himself – had told him that God is tough, hard and exacting. Someone had told him that God is akin to a "bookkeeper," an "auditor," a "big-brother" figure.

The servant had sadly misunderstood the nature of God. "God is to be feared like an enemy," he thinks. "God is out to get me," he surmises. In fact, the opposite is the truth. God is to be loved, because God is good. He expects faithfulness only in small things and then wants to entrust us with greater things. Mother Theresa of Calcutta had it right when she said, *"God expects us to be faithful, not successful."*

Ask the Holy Spirit now to enlighten you – to help you understand who God really is. It is said that St. Francis of Assisi used to stay awake for many hours each night asking

God two questions, *"God, who are you?" "And, who am I."* Jesus tells us the answer, *"God is your gentle, loving Father, and because you are his son – his daughter – have no fear, be not afraid."* This profound reality, that God is your Father and you his son or daughter will help you to board Christ's boat and serve humanity with a joyful spirit of service.

Casting aside fear and opening our hearts to Jesus as he walks by the Sea is totally worthwhile. Whether he calls us to Married Life, Priestly Life, Consecrated Life, Religious Life or Celibate Life in the Church, we shall discover that Christ is true to his promise: we will become *fishers of men.* Because of our response many will no longer live in the darkness of unbelief. Many will no longer fear death, but will discover a love that overcomes fear. Many will be healed of the paralysis of sin.

Remember, fishermen work from the boat – work that is mostly unseen. It is a work that requires great patience and skill. Sometimes the catch is paltry and pathetic. Other times the haul is immense and overwhelming. Fishermen work with others – it would be impossible to work alone. They work on the sea – both friend and foe. They surely work with love, realising that their work satisfies the hunger of the masses. They are in tune with the needs of others.

The boat, according to many an ancient Christian commentators, is a symbol of the Church. The sea, again according to many wise men, is a symbol of the world.

And so this is what it means to be called by Christ to be a fisherman – a fisher of men. It means working with others in the "boat" of the Church. It means we don't work alone, but work with a single mission in mind.

It requires patience. The haul of fish varies. Returns are not immediate. Fishing demands courage. The sea can be treacherous and the boat can be tossed this way and that.

But Christ is at the helm. It is his boat and the seas belong to him.

Stop and think about this great task of "fishing." Christ needs you and he calls you. Try and cast aside your fear and ambivalence. Try and enter this scene often. It takes time to become a successful *fisher of men*.

Flesh and Spirit

When Pope John Paul II was made a Bishop at the age of thirty-eight he took the motto, *Totus Tuus.* It means, "I am totally yours, Mary." He meant by this that he would be totally given to Christ, through Mary, the Mother of Christ. Mothers have a way of leading us in the right direction – subtlety and delicately – and Mary, the Mother of Jesus, is no exception.

We say, "blood is thicker than water." Family bonds are strong. It is true that they are not always easy, but family ties and connections are deep and abiding.

What is true for us is also true for Jesus. His mother and father would have taught him to talk and walk, to read and write, to love and laugh, to work and rest. Mary and Joseph would have held Jesus, kissed him and comforted him. Mary would have fed him at the breast.

As a Jewish boy, Mary and Joseph would have taught him about God. He would have lived perfectly the fourth commandment – *Honour your Father and Mother.* His love for Mary and Joseph would have been rich and constant.

And while Jesus grew in *wisdom and stature,* as St. Luke says in his Gospel, another family was developing. This was the family based not on blood, but on grace. Jesus was founding a family of the *Spirit* that would build on the family of the *flesh.*

St. Mark tells us about this in the last part of chapter three of his Gospel:

> *And his mother and his brethren came; and standing outside they sent to him and called him. And a crowd was sitting around him; and they said to him, "Your mother and your brethren are outside, asking for you." And he replied, "Who are my mother and my brethren?" And looking around on those who sat about him, he said, "Here are my mother and my brethren! Whoever does the will of God is my brother, and sister, and mother."*   (Mark 3, 31-35)

Mary of Nazareth was the Mother of Jesus according to the flesh. St. Luke tells us in his Gospel (*Luke 1, 26-38*) that the angel Gabriel appeared to Mary relaying a message from God. God wanted Mary to be the mother of Jesus according to the flesh. Mary was afraid, but with the angel's counsel agreed to the proposal put to her by God. She conceived Jesus by the power of the Holy Spirit without the intervention of man. And so Mary is called the *Virgin Mother of God.*

It was this *yes* to God's will that made Mary the Mother of Jesus according to the *Spirit.* Then, and only then, did she become the Mother of Jesus according to the *flesh*.

We human beings are exactly this: we are *spirit* and *flesh*. That is how we are constructed and that is how we are meant to function. Mary, the Mother of Jesus, functioned perfectly at both levels. She lived in Nazareth and had both feet on the ground. At the same time she lived with God as the first and most perfect disciple of Christ.

That is what Jesus says in the text of Mark. *"Here are my mother and my brothers. Anyone who does the will of God."* This is the true family of Jesus – the *Spirit-family* that listens to the word of God and does the will of God. Mary had good hearing – she listened attentively with the *ears* of her heart. Mary had good *hands* – she carried out the will of God in her hidden life in Nazareth by accepting to be the Mother of Jesus Christ. Mary is the disciple *par excellence* – a *hearer* and a *doer*.

The angel Gabriel had told Mary – to help her believe – that her cousin Elizabeth, despite her old age, had conceived the child she had longed desired. Mary set out as quickly as she could and went to Elizabeth. When Elizabeth greeted Mary she was inspired by the Holy Spirit and said: *"And why is this granted me, that the mother of my Lord should come to me?"* (Luke 1, 43).

We, too, can echo these sentiments. With Elizabeth we can ask ourselves, "Why am I so honoured that Mary, the Mother of the Lord, should come to visit me?" We take some time, now, to let the presence of *Our Lady* have some effect on our lives.

God had created Mary free of sin. By a singular grace she was *preserved* from Original Sin. Original is the sin of Adam and Eve. It is a sin of pride – wanting to be like God, knowing good and evil. And it affects us now. St. Paul gives us an insight into Original Sin and its effects when he says that we do the things we don't want to do and the things we want to do we often don't (Cf. *Romans 7, 15*).

Mary, however, was preserved from Original Sin. Christ's death and resurrection transcends time and space and so in his infinite wisdom and goodness he gifted Mary with a unique start – she was not burdened by Original Sin, as we are.

We call this Mary's *Immaculate Conception*. The Church teaches that Mary was conceived in the womb of her mother free from all sin – both original and personal. Furthermore, she remained free from sin for the whole of her life. That is, Mary never once transgressed the will of God. She was totally open and accommodating with God. Of course she was human and would have had conflicting emotions and feelings before the divine plan. But these realities do not amount to sin. Rather, she would have *felt* her feelings and emotions and then related them to God. So much so that she then desired what God desired. She is then the perfect disciple of Christ.

For this reason she is able to draw close to us in a unique way. Like no other human being, she is able to develop a friendship and intimacy that far outweighs what anyone else is able to do. In this Mary is *like* her Son, Jesus Christ. He is fully human and without sin. But then he is fully divine. In this Mary is *unlike* her Son. She is fully human, but not divine. Only Christ is both fully human and fully divine.

We can think about this for a moment, because what is being said here is rather important. Sin is what *divides* and *separates* people. It separates them from God, from each other and from themselves. Division is in some ways the history of humanity. We sin a lot. Sometimes we love to sin, other times we hate it, but sin is what we do!

Go back, when you have some spare moments, and read

the first two chapters of the *Book of Genesis* and then read chapter 3. The first two chapters give us some indication of what life would be like without sin. Chapter three then gives us an account of how sin entered the world. Importantly, it begins to indicate what sin brings into the world. Sin brings sin itself. It brings suffering. It carries death. The third chapter speaks of fear, accusation and division. In fact, the whole Bible gives us an account of division and how God comes to save and heal us of this terrible scar. But do have a read of the first three chapters of the *Book of Genesis* to satisfy your curiosity.

Now if sin brings division, separation and loneliness, imagine a person without sin. A person without sin, because she is not separated from us in any way, is able to draw close to us. Pope Benedict XVI said this much when referring to Mary's Immaculate Conception. On his visit to Lourdes in France in 2008 he said:

> *The privilege given to Mary, which sets her apart from our common condition, does not distance her from us, but on the contrary, it brings her closer. While sin divides, separating us from one another, Mary's purity makes her infinitely close to our hearts, attentive to each of us and desirous of our true good.*

If sin is worth thinking about for a few moments, this is worth meditating on for a lifetime! There is actually someone in human existence who is human, without sin and for that reason fully human. She actually shows us, through the witness of her life, what it means to be human.

Because she is without sin, she is able to draw close to our hearts, as Benedict XVI says, and furthermore, she is attentive to us and is desirous of our true good. She desires that we be as human as she is.

Let's imagine for a minute the *beauty* of this woman called Mary. Her *physical* beauty must be luminous, without comparison. Her eyes, her countenance, her whole physical disposition, must be breathtaking. When *Adam* in the *Book of Genesis* sees *Eve* for the first time he exclaims, "Ah, this at last is flesh of my flesh, bone of my bones" *(Genesis 2, 23). Eve* was beautiful and attracted *Adam's* attention.

God is the author of beauty. He is the *Beautiful One* beyond compare. He is indeed profoundly beautiful in himself and Mary, made in his image and likeness, free from all trace of sin, is surely patterned after his own beauty. We should not be afraid of beauty, nor confuse it with lust.

But now imagine the *interior* beauty of this woman called Mary. Imagine the beauty of her spirit, the beauty of her soul, the beauty of her heart, feelings and emotions, indeed the beauty of her entire being. We need this beauty in our lives. Indeed we need this beautiful woman in our lives, surrounded as we are, by so much ugliness.

In 1858 Mary appeared at Lourdes, in France, to a girl named Bernadette. Our Lady appeared to this young French girl over the course of a few days. Bernadette was asked who the "Lady" was that was appearing to her. She could not confirm who it was, but said that "she was the most beautiful woman she had ever seen."

Go back now to St. Luke's account of Mary's visit to her cousin Elizabeth. You will find it in chapter 1. Take some time to be in the house with Elizabeth. Situate yourself in that house so that you don't disturb their meeting, but be close enough so that you can hear what is being said. Make sure you are close enough to catch a glimpse of Mary's beauty.

Use all of your senses. See what is going on. See the joy in their faces. Watch them embrace. Hear them speak words of wonder, love and joy to each other. Listen to their conversation, which lasted for three months. Hear how they describe to each other the mystery of God's action and presence in their lives. Sense their faith. Smell the food cooking – and taste it! Touch them occasionally and feel the environment around you. They won't mind if you stay for a few days or longer if you want to.

Mary, the Mother of our Lord, is also very much *our* Mother. This prayer, called the *Sub Tuum*, is one of the earliest prayers we have to Mary. It's worth learning off by heart and repeating it often. Mary will help you come closer to Christ – Son of Mary and Son of God – for that is our greatest need.

> ### Sub Tuum
> *We fly to your patronage,*
> *O Holy Mother of God.*
> *Despise not our petitions in our necessities,*
> *but deliver us from all dangers,*
> *O ever-glorious and blessed Virgin. Amen*

Rich Soil

The Mother of God received the Word of God in faith and brought forth the baby Jesus in Bethlehem. She gave birth to the *Bread of Life* in the town commonly known as the *House of Bread.* She provided "rich soil" for the seed of faith.

The Word of God is the seed that God desires to sow in each of us. Jesus' preferred method of teaching was parables and the parable to end all parables is the parable of the sower. Jesus says so himself. When his disciples ask Jesus to explain the parable, he says to them, *"Do you not understand this parable? Then how will you understand any of the parables?"*

Again, Jesus is near the Sea of Galilee, he climbs into a boat, opens his mouth and teaches the multitude:

> *Listen! A sower went out to sow. And as he sowed, some seed fell along the path, and the birds came and*

> *devoured it. Other seed fell on rocky ground, where it
> had not much soil, and immediately it sprang up, and
> since it had no depth of soil; and when the sun rose it
> was scorched, and since it had no root it withered away.
> Other seed fell among thorns and the thorns grew up
> and choked it, and it yielded no grain. And other seeds
> fell into good soil and brought forth grain, growing up
> and increasing and yielding thirtyfold and sixtyfold
> and hundredfold. And he said, "He who has ears to
> hear, let him hear." (Mark 4, 3-9)*

Jesus implores us to "hear" – to listen. So, too, does the great commandment to love God as found in the *Book of Deuteronomy* in the Old Testament:

> *"Hear, O Israel: The Lord our God is one Lord; and
> you shall love the Lord your God with all your heart,
> and with all your soul, and with all your might.
> (Deuteronomy 6, 4)*

Loving God with all of our heart, soul and might is not possible if we don't listen. The Lord our God is *One*. This does not mean that God is numerically one, but rather that he is a *Unity* of persons – a communion of love between three persons. The Father, Son and Holy Spirit are *One* – they are distinct, but inseparable. They are completely unified in their existence. They are *One*.

And this is what God desires for us. He desires that all that makes up our life – the spirit, the flesh – be brought into great harmony. He desires that we be unified – that we be one.

For this reason we need to listen to our true selves. We need to listen to those who are true witnesses. We need to listen to the *Crucified* and *Risen One*. And this is no easy task. Listening is extremely difficult in our *noise-riddled culture*.

Noise, not music, is all around us. Noise, not conversation, is the reality. Noise, not silence, is contemporary man's constant companion. Surely atheism – the denial of God – finds its roots in a *noise-riddled culture*? God speaks, but because clatter and noise fills our interior and exterior atmosphere we are unable to hear the voice of God.

And so Jesus calls us, urges us and compels us to listen. Try and find some of that *blessed silence* that Jesus lives so well. Mark tells us in no uncertain terms that Jesus was a man who sought after silence so that he could commune with his Father.

As Jesus embarked upon his public ministry he found himself surrounded by needy people. He finds himself in great demand for healings of one sort or another. But he needs his space and so he goes and gets it:

> *And in the morning, a great while before day, he rose*
> *and went out to a lonely place, and there he prayed.*
> *(Mark 1, 35)*

The alarm clock goes off and we rise before the sun rises. We find a place so that we can listen to Christ. We might even be able to get to morning Mass before work begins? At this early morning hour the brain is foggy, but this does not stop us from hearing what the Lord has to say to us. We receive light and encouragement for the day ahead. Our conscience may be pricked for something we had done or failed to do the day before. We finish with a simple resolution to be more faithful to Christ. God has spoken – we have listened. We have become rich soil for the seed who is Christ.

Despite our advances in science we still really don't understand the mystery of the seed falling into the ground, dying, and rising to become fruitful. Jesus sees in this mystery something of the mystery of human life and its dynamic of dying and rising. In fact, he uses it as a metaphor to describe his own life – his kingdom.

> *And he said, "The kingdom of God is as if a man should scatter seed upon the ground, and should sleep and rise night and day, and the seed should sprout and grow, he knows not how. The earth produces of itself, first the blade, then the ear, then the full grain in the ear. But when the grain is ripe, at once he puts in the sickle, because the harvest has come." (Mark 4, 26-29)*

> *And he said, "With what can we compare the kingdom of God, or what parable shall we use for it? It is like a grain of mustard seed, which, when sown upon the ground, is the smallest of all the seeds on earth; yet when it is sown it grows up and becomes the greatest of all the shrubs, and puts forth large branches, so that the birds of the air can make nests in its shade." (Mark 4, 30-32)*

Jesus speaks about this *natural* mystery because he lives the divine mystery of dying and rising. He himself falls to the ground. He dies. He rises and reveals to us his glorious resurrection. The harvest is indeed rich.

Let us ask the Lord for humility. Falling to the ground and dying is no easy thing. But it is totally necessary that we follow this path marked out by the Lord. The promise is not just a wonderful harvest in this life. The promise is an eternal, glorious resurrected life, beyond anything we can ever imagine.

Jesus says to us, *"Listen! Hear!"* Let's take some time to do just that. In this way we will come to understand, in some sort of fashion, the mystery of the seed. And we will come to understand why it important to become "rich soil."

The Rhythm of God

To most peoples' total surprise the Bible states that God *works* and *rests*. To declare that God works is not all that surprising. To say that God rests, however, sounds a bit dubious.

We live in a culture where long hours of work are the norm for almost everyone. This perhaps is the reason why people are somewhat taken aback when Jews and Christians alike say that God rests as well as works.

In fact, the Bible seems to place a higher value on rest than it does on work. For the *Book of Genesis* states clearly that God created the world in seven days. For six days he worked and then he rested on the seventh day. But the Bible says explicitly that God had not finished his work of creation until he rested. Have a read of the first chapter of the *Book of Genesis* and discover this truth.

So, God's activity is both working and resting. *God is love,* says St. John in his First Letter. Thus, working and resting are for God expressions of his love.

But why and how does rest finish or perfect the work that God had done in his creation? It is a very good question and one I suspect that most people would struggle to answer.

The answer is quite simple and for that reason quite profound. God rested on the seventh day so that he could *contemplate* the work he had done. By resting, God was able to "look back" or "look over" his creative work and declare it good. By doing this he finished his work. What tradesman, for instance, who takes pride in his work, doesn't look back at his work with joy and pleasure? What mother or father, when their son or daughter graduates from college, doesn't relax after the event and chat about what has been achieved? Our "business" is not finished until we stop and review. Until we rest and reflect.

And so we, made in God's image and likeness, are called to do exactly what God does: work for a time, and then, take time to rest so that we can look back at our work, *internalise* it and therefore finish it. When we stop and contemplate the work that we have done, we are able to sense the goodness of what has been achieved. We are able to sense the *hand of God* in what we have been doing. In other words, we come to a deeper understanding of God's providence. We begin to understand something of the mystery of work – that work is in fact both a human and divine activity.

Once again, Jesus shows us the way forward in this matter. His words are confirmed by his actions, for after honouring the Sabbath Day by worshipping his Father he decides to take the disciples on a walk to teach them the importance of rest. He heads down to the cornfields. St. Mark describes the scene:

> *One sabbath he was going through the grainfields; and*

*as they made their way his disciples began to pluck ears
of grain. And the Pharisees said to him, "Look, why are
they doing what is not lawful on the sabbath? And he
said to them, "Have you never read what David did,
when he was in need and was hungry, he and those
who were with him: how he entered the house of God,
when Abi'athar was high priest, and ate the bread of the
Presence, which it is not lawful for any but the priests
to eat, and also gave it to those who were with him?"
And he said to them, "The sabbath was made for man,
not man for the sabbath; so the Son of man is lord even
of the sabbath."*   (Mark 2, 23-28)

The Sabbath day was close to the heart of the Jewish
people. It was understood to be a day of worship and rest.
You can imagine what happened here. Jesus says to his
disciples, "Let's go and have a look at the crop." The field
was probably planted by one of them or at least by a good
friend or relative. So off they go. The crop is so good that
they decide to help themselves to it.

The Pharisees raise an objection. They think that this type
of activity is forbidden on the Sabbath. But they are wrong.
What they had done over successive generations was to focus
on the law *itself*, rather than look to the specific human *value*
that the law was preserving and promoting. They failed to
look *beyond* the law, to see its *purpose*.

This sort of misunderstanding happens in our own day.
We have laws against speeding, not because driving fast is a
sin, but because it helps protect lives from fatal car crashes.
We have to look beyond the law to see what is really at
stake.

And that is what Jesus does. He gives them the concrete
example of King David's need and then finishes by saying,
"*The Sabbath was made for man, not man for the Sabbath.*" In

other words, the Sabbath is a day of worship and rest to help man live according to his nature. The law of the Sabbath is there to help us be true human beings.

Now all of this is relevant to life in the 21st Century, because for many people work has become a form of slavery. People feel trapped, not only in their work, but also in their very lives. Even our weekends have become overrun with a plethora of activities. There's no time to catch our breath. We seem to stumble from one thing to another, with little time for thought, reflection or rest. There even seems little time for each other. People live in the same house, but they might as well be ships passing in the night.

And yet our work and our lives are meant to be expressions of love and freedom. Interestingly enough, there are two words in the Latin language for work. One is *labor* and the other is *opus*. The meaning of the former is easy enough to guess. It indicates the toil of work, the labour of work, the exhaustion of work. We can certainly identify with this.

But the word *opus* is less familiar. It is the word that great composers use for their musical masterpieces. Artists use it, too, for their wonderful creations on canvas. In fact, it is the word we use for God's work of creation. God did not work in a laborious sense when he made the world. Rather, his work of creating the world out of nothing was an *opus*.

The word then indicates a generous, fruitful, overflowing, free and inspired work. It is a work that is totally gratuitous and the result of an inner freedom on the part of God. His work is thus an act of love – the result of his love for humanity.

If we imitate God's way of doing things – working and resting – we, too, will come to this understanding of our work. Our work will be transformed from what can appear at times to be a form of slavery – at least a form of compulsion

– into an act of freedom and love.

The toil of work will never disappear – that is true. But what will appear is a new vision of work and life. But it will only make its appearance in our lives if we rest and contemplate our work. In this we become like the *One* who made us.

Go back to that scene in Mark's Gospel frequently. It will be more than helpful in giving direction to your life. Try and make Sunday – the Christian Sabbath – a day of worship and rest. Try and see Sunday, not as the day that helps you prepare for the upcoming week, or as a day to do nothing, but rather as the day that God gives you to help you finish your work.

Find some time to think about the past week. What is the quality of your work? Do you see it as a participation in God's work of creation? Is God the chief partner in your work, or do you work alone? Try and think about the people you work with and the ways you can be a better witness to them. Think about your motivations, too. Is my work done for the benefit of others or is it yet another banal and pointless attempt to build up my own sense of self-importance?

In other words, struggle to see Sunday as the day that it really is – God's weekly gift to you to help you live that rhythm of working and resting. It is the rhythm of the Creator and it is a good space to be in.

Night Clubs

In chapter six of his Gospel, St. Mark describes an horrific event – the beheading of John the Baptist:

> *For Herod had sent and seized John, and bound him in prison for the sake of Hero'di-as, his brother Philip's wife; because he had married her. For John said to Herod, "It is not lawful for you to have your brother's wife." And Hero'di-as had a grudge against him, and wanted to kill him. But she could not, for Herod feared John, knowing that he was a righteous and holy man, and kept him safe. When he heard him, he was much perplexed; and yet he heard him gladly.*

> *But an opportunity came when Herod on his birthday gave a banquet for his courtiers and officers and the leading men of Galilee. For when Hero'di-as' daughter came in and danced, she pleased Herod and his guests;*

*and the king said to the girl, "Ask me for whatever
you wish, and I will grant it." And he vowed to her,
"Whatever you ask me, I will give you, even half of my
kingdom." And she went out, and said to her mother,
"What shall I ask ?" And she said, "The head of John
the Baptiser."* (Mark 6, 17-24)

The girl went to Herod with her request. The king, afraid of
losing respect among his peers by reneging on his ridiculous
promise, granted her wish. And that was that.

Notice what is happening here. John the Baptist is the
first person in the New Testament to consciously shed his
blood for Jesus. He is the last and greatest prophet to bear
witness to Jesus and he bears witness to him by offering his
very life. Indeed, that word martyr means just that – to "bear
witness."

But notice, too, that John not only gives his life for
Jesus. In fact, he gives his life for the Church's teaching on
marriage. He is beheaded because he upholds the sanctity
of marriage. He appeals to Herod's conscience for taking
his brother's wife – Herodias – to himself in an illicit and
immoral marriage. John was not going to remain silent. That
was not his style. Only false prophets keep their mouths shut
and their tongues tied. John was not going to be intimidated
by Herod. And so it was. He shed his blood for Christ.

And what about us? What is our thinking about marriage
these days? Is it just an old fashioned institution, no longer
relevant for the 21st Century? Is marriage merely a piece
of paper, no different really to living together in a *defacto*
relationship? Is it something that the state or government can
dissolve or dismantle at the whim of just one of the parties
to the marriage? We can be tempted to think like this, living
as we are, in a society where marital break up seems to be
the norm.

But the truth is otherwise. For the Jewish people and for many people down the ages, marriage is intimate and sacred. The *Book of Genesis* tells us that *Adam*, upon seeing *Eve*, exclaimed: *"This at last is bone of my bones and flesh of my flesh"* (Genesis 2, 23). And having laid his eyes upon her beauty, he decided to surrender his heart and become *one flesh* with her: *"Therefore a man leaves his father and his mother and cleaves to his wife, and they become one flesh"* (Genesis 2, 24).

All great cultures and societies are built on the "rock" of marriage. Think about this:

> Marriage is the *basis of family* and family is the *basis of society*.

When a husband and wife treasure their friendship and become soul mates great things happen, not only to them, but also to their children. The love of husband and wife has a *ripple effect*. They themselves grow and develop as great human beings. The experience of unity in marriage leads husband and wife to a new awareness of dignity and identity.

The Bible calls friendship an *elixir* – a "soothing tonic." That is exactly what a good marriage is for husband and wife. Their marriage *massages* their body, soul and spirit, and it effects – profoundly – the fruit of their marital love. Their children feel secure and loved when they experience this love. They too receive a "soothing tonic" in preparation for their life's journey.

John the Baptist had got it right. When people 'play' with marriage, they are playing with fire. When people profane marriage, they get burnt. John was stating the truth for the benefit, not only of Herod, but also for Herodias. She couldn't see it. Herod sensed it, but was too weak to act on it.

Part of his weakness came from his dissipated life. Ancient

thinkers understood that there exist four *cardinal virtues*. The word cardinal comes from the Latin language and means "hinge." In other words, life "swings" on these *hinge virtues*. Think of a door. The hinges enable you to open it and close it. The same is true with our lives. The success of our lives are dependent upon whether we *close* the door on things that are going to distract us and upon whether we are going to *open* the door on matters that will lead us to walk the right path.

The four cardinal virtues are:

> *Prudence*
> *Temperance*
> *Fortitude*
> *Justice*

We need to be prudent – to think before we act. We need to exercise temperance – to be balanced in our use of material things. We must have fortitude – not to be afraid of doing or saying the right thing. We need to be just – to give to others what is due to them.

The beheading of John the Baptist all started with a party. You can imagine the scene: Plenty of food; bucket loads of alcohol; women dressed scantily; men on the "lookout;" comfortable lounges, seductive music - a seductive atmosphere where anything can happen. It all sounds like a modern day nightclub.

Herod has plenty to drink and gets aroused by a young woman – the daughter, in fact, of his illicit wife – who comes and dances impurely before him. This is not the recognition of beauty that *Adam* experienced when he sighted *Eve*, but lust. He loses his reason and from there we know the story.

Herod lost control. He was intemperate and impure. Then he was imprudent, weak and cowardly, and unjust. It all started, we remind ourselves, with too much to drink!

Several years ago now, I went to buy a cigar to celebrate my nephew's twenty-first birthday. I entered what I thought was a regular hotel. I was half way into the building when I realised that it was, in fact, a nightclub. I was a little taken aback, but undeterred I went looking for a cigar.

I came to the main bar of the nightclub. The music was pulsating. The place was packed with young people. The smell of alcohol was in the air and there was a haze, too, from illicit substances. I stood in line, waiting to ask for the prized cigar. And then a young woman caught sight of me and said to me, "*Father*, what are *you* doing here?" Instinctively, I said to her, "*And* what are *you* doing here?"

Indeed, what are young people doing wasting their lives in nightclubs where they set themselves up to lose everything they should cherish: their minds, their senses, their hearts, their virginity, their friendships, their families?

What path are you on? And what of your friends? Is it the path that leads to light and life or the path that dead-ends with darkness and death? A lot depends on the company you keep. A lot depends on the "doors" that you *open* and the "doors" that you *close*.

Walk through the ones that are open and turn your back on the ones that you close. While you are at it, help many of your friends to do the same. Christ expects this of you because you are human. You are not a "sheep." Sheep follow. Human beings lead.

Tough decisions must be made and there are critical moments in life when we have to make them. Don't sit on the fence. Be decisive. Abundant fruit will follow.

Dying and Rising

I am dying. And so are you. I will die. And so will you. Nothing is more certain. No one can stop it.

What do we make of it? Well, you either believe that death is the end – the complete end. Or, you believe that death is not the end, but a beginning. Death is a *passage* or a *passing over* to a new kind of life. In this case, you would believe that there is life beyond the grave.

So, if you believe that death is the end, then that is that. There is nothing more to life than death, since death has the last say. At some point you come into existence. You live your life for a few years – maybe eighty or ninety if you are lucky – and then it is terminated. You die. You no longer are. You simply disappear back to nothing. In other words, death is death. The only thing that would remain is the memory that others have of you – if you're lucky.

If you believe this, then you are an atheist – someone who does not believe in God. Actually, an atheist is a bit more than that. For the word itself is a Greek word which literally means, "against God." At any rate, an atheist is someone who does not believe that God created the world with a purpose. It all happened by chance or it just happened and it will all just go away. Life is a mirage. It has no meaning.

It is, as you can see, a radical position, and you would want to have some very sound reasons for believing it.

Just stop for a moment and think this through. An atheist – a person who does not believe in life after death – takes a radical *philosophical* position. For what he or she is saying – if they stop and think about it – is quite disturbing.

Essentially he or she would be thinking: "There was a time when I was not. I did not exist at all. Now I exist. I live my life. But then I die. I will no longer exist." In other words, "I was not, I am, I will not be."

Does this make any sense on a philosophical level? That is, does it make any sense if I think about it reasonably? The answer must surely be no. Why? Because it is simply absurd to think that *life is a preparation for death*! That life is an *antechamber*.

Think about this, "I was not, I am, I will not be." So, I have life, so that I may die. I have something, so that I will have nothing. This is simply ridiculous. Why not just be nothing and be done with it? Why have life at all? Why would there be life if it is preceded by nothing and is succeeded by nothing? In fact, if there was nothing, and will be nothing, then there should be nothing! But, there is *something*. So, life must be a preparation for something, not nothing. That makes infinite more sense.

This is why really great thinkers, like John Henry Newman, understood clearly that unbelief and denial of the afterlife arises from a defect of the *heart*, not of the *intellect*. Atheism has its roots, not in *reason* as such, but in some *wound* in a person's heart.

On the other hand, if you are a believer – of some sorts – then you believe that death is not the end. That beyond death there is life. The believer does not know a lot of detail about life after death, but he or she is fairly convinced that "life is changed, not ended."

Believing in life after death does not mean that believers trivialise death. On the contrary, death is a very difficult thing – particularly when it comes unexpectedly to the unsuspecting. Death will be difficult for all of us, no matter how much faith we have. Why? Because we fear death – at least in some way. Death is not something with which we are familiar. We haven't died before and we will only die once. The unknown tends to produce fear.

Christ has promised us that he has gone ahead to prepare a place for us. That is true. But there is still a lot we don't know about death and life beyond it. We have not had the experience of death. We have not had the experience of a life different to the one we now have.

The Bible is rather candid about all of this. In the Old Testament the prophet *Isaiah* tells us:

> *On this mountain the Lord of hosts will make for all peoples a feast of fat things, a feast of wine on the lees, of fat things full of marrow, of wine on the lees well refined.*
>
> *And he will destroy on this mountain the covering that is cast over all peoples, the veil that is spread over all nations. He will swallow up death forever, and the Lord*

*will wipe away tears from all faces, and the reproach of
his people he will take away from all the earth; for the
Lord has spoken.*(Isaiah 25, 6-8)

Death brings sorrow and hence "tears." The prophet is
right – death is difficult and painful as we watch it unfold.
Death disturbs.

But then he also describes death as a "covering" or "veil."
That makes sense, too. For a veil covers something. We know
there is something there, but we can't quite see it clearly. We
can't quite "get a hold on it." In other words, as believers we
believe in life after death, but death casts a shadow or veil
over the matter. We can't quite "see" what is beyond death.

And now the promise: God "will swallow up death
forever" and he "will wipe away tears from all faces." Death
will not have the last say, as it so often appears to have.

So death is real, but so is the promise of life beyond death.
"I was not, I am, I will be." Life is not a preparation for death.
Something is not a preparation for nothing. Beyond life – and
death – there is another life.

But death will come, with its pain, its rupture and
disintegration. Body and soul will separate at the point of
death and that will not be all that easy.

If, however, we die a little each day to ourselves, then our
death will be like a "sister" – as St. Francis of Assisi liked to
say. A "sister" means a welcome companion. As the saying
goes, "don't try and do in half an hour what you should have
been doing your whole life long – dying to your self." If we
do die to ourselves, then our death will be welcome. We will
be embraced by the mercy of Christ.

What is "dying to self?" It is not thinking selfishly about
"me." It is putting others before me. It is "dying" so that
others may be "rising." Why die to self? It is a beautiful
thing to do. To think first of others and only then of oneself

is liberating. We find happiness in serving others – by being kind to them.

Also, we need to "die to self" because sin has entered the world and the consequence of sin is death. Sin has many consequences, but death is the ultimate price we pay for sin. And if we are honest with ourselves, we can see many forms of death in our lives: personal and social disharmonies of one sort or another, tensions, signs of decay, alienation, lust, domination, hostility, etc. It is all there to see if we but open our eyes and admit the truth.

Christ came to confront this reality. He came to embrace death so as to destroy it. As we have already noted, "Christ put death to death by his death." That is to say, Christ's death is a death to sin. It is an entirely unique death. His wounds were my wounds. His death is my death. And so his death heals my death. He puts my death to death by his death. He rises from the dead so that I may rise from the dead. He gives me a new resurrected life – not just an eternal life – where all things will be made new. I will be new and different.

It is for this reason that he often told his disciples that they must "deny themselves, take up their cross and follow him." They must die to sin and so let their true, hidden selves arise.

This is what is at stake in life: Either I die to myself and bear much fruit or I refuse to die and remain alone. If I die, then I rise and I rise with many others. My life expands. If, on the other hand, I refuse to die, then my life contracts, dwindles and ultimately self-destructs.

The choice is Christ or self. If we choose Christ, then we die to our *old* self and emerge with the *new* and *true* self. If we go the other way, then the *old* self eventually dies and rots away. Loneliness is the fruit of an unwillingness to die.

> *Truly, truly, I say to you, unless a grain of wheat falls into the earth and dies, it remains alone; but if it dies, it bears much fruit. (John 12, 24)*

Take these rather radical thoughts to your prayer life. Read the passion, death and resurrection of Jesus in the Gospel. Mark begins it at chapter 14 of his Gospel.

To read the Lord's passion, death and resurrection, and to enter into it – to live it – is the most important thing we can do in life. For it answers perfectly the riddle every human person must ultimately face – the riddle of death and the mystery of rising to a new life.

Miracles and Madness

St. Mark tells us that on two occasions Jesus fed a large number of people with just a few loaves and fishes. The first time we are told that he fed five thousand people. The second time we are told that he fed four thousand. St. Mark seems to indicate that the first miracle was for the Jewish people, while the second prodigious miracle was for the Gentiles – the rest of the world. After the crowd had had their fill, the disciples gathered up the remains. The leftovers were greater than the original quantity. The whole thing seemed surreal.

And that of course is the point. I remember catechising young people in preparation for their first Holy Communion. I explained to the children that when you go to Mass the bread is turned into the body of Christ and the wine is changed into the blood of Christ. One of the children, a little boy who was a little rough around the edges, said to me, "That's ridiculous." I said to him, "You're dead right."

Christ worked many miracles. He cast out demons; he gave sight to the blind; he healed the sick; he raised people from the dead; he walked on water; he calmed storms. Tell someone about these miracles and they will tell you that you are mad.

What are we to make of them? For one thing, Christ gave them as *signs* to the people to help them believe in him. But that is what they are – *signs* – and not *proofs* of Christ's divinity. Two people can see and experience a miracle and yet they may come to entirely different conclusions. One may come to believe in Christ, while the other may remain perplexed, sceptical and indifferent.

The sign does not stand-alone. Rather, it goes hand in hand with the *words* spoken by Jesus. Both are meant to evoke faith. The sign *confirms* the words, while the words *interpret* the sign. The sign is for *sight*. The word is for *heart*. Remember, we humans are both *flesh* and *spirit*. We need signs and words. We need both to believe.

A second thing about miracles: We live in a world created by God. It has a rhythm that is sort of miraculous. It has a beauty that stimulates and inspires. We believe, of course, that God created it from nothing by speaking his Word.

Now suppose the *One* who created it actually enters it – what might we expect? Something likes miracles – I suspect. For the *Creator* has entered his *creation*, not to play with it or to manipulate it, but to *heal* it and *raise* it up. The *supernatural* enters the *natural*. It is the *Spirit* entering the *flesh*. When this happens we get miracles. It happened in Christ's time and it happens now – on a daily basis.

Miracles, in fact, are acts of love. The Creator loves his creation. The Creator loves his creatures and so he is not content to leave his creatures on their own. He comes to heal the sick; cast out demons; raise the dead to life; turn water in wine; turn wine into his blood. The *Uncreated One* is in love with the *created one*. He is the *Lover* in love with his *beloved*. And that creature, that beloved, is you and I.

This is why Jesus worked these miracles of the loaves and fishes. He was providing for the material needs of the people who were tired and hungry. They did not have enough money or time to get what they needed for their physical sustenance. Jesus had compassion on them and fed them.

Now the interesting point about the miracle, besides the sheer size of it, is that Jesus was preparing his disciples for another miracle that would have far reaching significance throughout history. He was preparing them for the miracle that we call the *Eucharist*. Jesus was preparing the disciples for the miracle of his body and blood to be celebrated in the Church down through the ages.

How do we know this? St. Mark and the other Gospel writers tell us so. Go and read the miracles of the loaves – *Mark 6, 30-44* and *Mark 8, 1-10.* Jesus initially tells the disciples to feed the crowd, knowing full well that they simply don't have the means with which to feed them. In other words, he wants to evoke in them a desire to care for the crowd, to minister to their needs, to be a father to them, to be like a *Good Shepherd* who tends and watches over his flock. So he says, *"You give them something to eat yourselves,"* knowing full well that they can't do it.

Notice, too, how St. Mark describes the miracle: He says that Jesus *took* bread; he *blessed* it; *broke* it; he *gave* it to the disciples to share among the crowd. He took, blessed, broke and gave. This is exactly the same language that is used of

Jesus at the Last Supper. While he was at supper he took the bread, said the blessing over the bread, broke it and gave it to his disciples, telling them that they should *"Do this in memory of Me"* (cf. *Luke 22, 19*).

Let's put it like this: St. Mark, through the eyes of St. Peter, saw what Jesus did in both miracles of the loaves and fishes. He saw the same type of behaviour at the *Last Supper*. He noticed a *pattern* in Jesus' actions – in his way of doing things. Mark understood the connection between the events and so made it clear in his description, both of the miracle of the loaves and fishes and of the *Last Supper*.

In other words, the miracle of the loaves was a *prefigurement* of the Last Supper. It was a preparatory event. To be sure, multiplying loaves and fishes is one thing – turning bread and wine into the Body and Blood of Christ is quite another. But nevertheless, the miracle of the loaves prefigures and therefore prepares us for the extraordinary miracle of the Eucharist. Hence the language: Jesus took, blessed, broke and gave the bread.

Given this, what do we believe about the Eucharist? What has the Church taught down the centuries? What is the tradition? What has she tried to "hand over" to successive generations?

St. Matthew, St. Mark, St. Luke and St. Paul all tell us that at the *Last Supper*, Jesus took bread and wine and turned it into his Body and Blood. Furthermore, he told them *"Do this in memory of me."* St. John for his part does not include this scene in his Gospel.

Why not, I hear you ask? It seems that he preferred in his Gospel to give an account of Jesus' teaching on the matter in chapter six of his Gospel. There Jesus calls himself the *Bread of Life* and says clearly that unless we eat his flesh and drink his blood we will not have life within us. John also was the last to write his Gospel and knew, it seems, that the others had already given account of the *Last Supper*. So he decided to focus on the washing of the disciples feet at the *Last Supper*. You can read this in chapter thirteen of his Gospel.

So bread becomes the Body of Christ and wine becomes his Blood, and furthermore, the apostles are given the express command to repeat this ritualistic action. Because the Bible is so clear about this – all four Gospel writers and St. Paul agree unanimously about it – the Church has always taught this truth.

So, let there be no doubt. The Eucharist is the Body and Blood of Christ. That is, when a person receives Holy Communion at Mass they receive the Body, Blood, Soul and Divinity of Christ!

That's it. No mistake, no debate - only a desire to enter into this mystery with humility. What looks like a little wafer bread – no bigger than a twenty-cent coin – is in fact Jesus Christ. Now that is madness, but that is what happens when the Creator enters his creation – when the supernatural mingles with the natural.

Furthermore, as St. Paul makes abundantly clear, when the Body and Blood of Christ are present so too is his sacrificial death and glorious resurrection. *"Greater love,"* says St. John, *"has no man than this, that a man lay down his life for his friends"* *(John 15, 13)*. And that is what Christ does for us – he lays down his life. He sacrifices his own life for love of us. And this mysterious self-offering is *made present* when bread and wine is transformed into Christ's Body and Blood.

And this too seems madness. We all have memories and memories make present, in some fashion, past events. God, too, has a memory and it is so perfect that when he remembers, past events become present in reality. Some people are said to have photographic memories. God's memory is like this, but infinitely more. When he remembers, past events actually become present.

This is exactly what happens when Catholic Mass is celebrated. The priest, acting in the person of Christ, remembers Christ's death and resurrection. But it is Christ's memory that the priest makes his own. It is Christ's memory that the Church makes her own. That is what we are called to do: *make Christ's memory our own. Lest we forget!*

The *remembering* of Jesus is so real and powerful that it *makes present* his death and resurrection. This happens by *means* of what we call the *consecration* of the bread and wine into Christ's Body and Blood. Thus we are present at his death and resurrection when we pray at Mass.

This mysterious reality – Christ's death and resurrection – is *made present* by means of a sacrament. A sacrament is a visible sign of an invisible reality. Bread is the visible sign. The Body of Christ is the invisible reality. Wine is the visible sign. The Blood of Christ is the invisible reality. Thus the Church teaches clearly, and without any doubt whatsoever, that the *appearances* of bread and wine remain, but the *substance* – that is, the actual reality – is Christ's Body and Blood. We see a wafer of bread, but we worship and receive the Body of Christ; we taste what appears to be wine, but we drink his Blood. This is the truth.

St. Thomas Aquinas said that the Eucharist *was* the greatest miracle that Christ worked. We can add: it *is* the greatest miracle that Christ works. It is indeed a *miracle of madness*. At every Mass we are present at Christ's passion, death, resurrection and ascension. Furthermore, we have the opportunity - if we are correctly disposed - to receive the Body and Blood of Christ whom we adore at each Mass.

The Church teaches us that the Eucharist is the *source* and *summit* of our lives. What does that mean? How can we make this a reality?

Let's go back to that miracle of the loaves and fishes. We noticed that Christ "took," "blessed," "broke" and "gave" the loaves and fishes to the disciples to give to the people. But then isn't this what Jesus did during his passion and death? Didn't he allow himself to be "taken," "broken" and "given" for our salvation. The soldiers "took" him - they mocked him, scourged him, crowned him with thorns. In this they "broke" his body. In this Jesus allowed himself to be "given" for us. And by offering this suffering to his Father on our behalf, he allowed himself to be "blessed."

This is Jesus' way of acting. He "takes," "blesses," "breaks" and "gives" the loaves and fishes. He has the same pattern of behaviour at the *Last Supper* - he takes bread, blesses, breaks and give his Body and Blood to the needy disciples. He then let's this happen to his very person in his suffering and death. In other words, he carries out on Good Friday what he performed in ritualistic form on the night of the *Last Supper*.

And so we get the hint. Jesus is asking us: "Will you allow yourself to be 'taken' and 'blessed' by me?" "Will you allow yourself to be 'broken' and 'given' for the life of the world?" "Will you follow me in my way of acting?" "Will you be my disciples?" This is how we live the Eucharist. We let Christ put these questions to us – on a daily basis.

Down through the ages the Eucharist has always had key elements. The believers gather in one place. They listen to the Word of God. They offer themselves with bread and wine. They worship the sacred Body and precious Blood of the Lord. They approach the altar to receive Christ's Body and Blood. Finally, they go in peace.

To live the Eucharist means that we allow ourselves to be gathered with others who are followers of Christ and so sense the mystery of the Body of Christ - the Church.

Then we allow ourselves to penetrated by the Word of God. Christ speaks to us through the words of the Old and New Testament. Christ encourages us, he enlivens us, he challenges us - with his Word. Heart speaks to heart. Then we profess our faith and pray for the world. We then offer ourselves with the bread and wine. We let ourselves be taken up into Christ's perfect love - an act of offering and sacrifice for us. We prepare ourselves to receive back Jesus' Body and Blood in Communion.

And then the priest offers a short, pithy dismissal, which is full of light and meaning. "Go in peace," he says, "to love and serve the Lord." We depart full of grace to *live* what we have just *celebrated*. Christ encourages us: "You have let yourselves be 'taken' and 'blessed' by me at this Mass, now go and let yourselves be 'broken' and 'given' for the life of the world."

This is what it means to live the Eucharist - to make it the source and summit of our lives:

> *To be "taken" so that others may be "freed."*
> *To be "blessed" so that others may be "called."*
> *To be "broken" so that others may be "healed."*
> *To be "given" so that others may "receive."*
> *To "die" so that others may "rise."*

Solitude and Silence

The Holy Spirit threw Jesus into the wilderness for forty days and forty nights. It was a time of temptation and testing. But it was also a time of fasting and prayer.

As you read the Gospels over and over again, you will notice this trait of Jesus: he likes to get away by himself to pray. He wants to be intimate with his Father. And the Spirit places this same desire deep within us. You may have suppressed it. You may have repressed it. Either way, the desire will always remain, because that is how we are built.

We need solitude and silence. Not as an end in themselves, but rather as a means to an end. We need solitude and silence to listen to the heart: the heart of Christ and our own hearts.

When we stop and take some silence, we hear the noise. The noise is "within" and the noise is "without." The world is busy. The world is noisy. And to be honest, there is a certain energy about it all. We like to be busy. We enjoy the pace and get a kick out of it. But it leaves us dissatisfied. It leaves a "bad taste in our mouths." We get sick and tired of it. We sense that we need to take a break. We need some time to be by ourselves and to be with the Lord.

But then there is noise "within." There is a noise in our very being. We take time out and get some silence, but we still hear the inner noise. We come to realise that there are many voices within. There are many conflicting emotions and feelings within. There is a multitude of thoughts within. We feel ill at ease. Inner peace escapes us. And this is true, despite our best efforts to try and retreat from the noise.

The noise that we discover within has been acknowledged by many people. It is the reason why all great religions – not just the Christian religion – try to encourage their members to retreat from everyday life and to be silent so that they can listen to the movements of the heart.

Take for instance a man like St. Anthony of Egypt – commonly accepted as the founder of Christian monasticism. Historians agree that he lived to the ripe old age of one hundred and five. He was born in 251AD and died in 356AD. He lived the life of a hermit in the desert. Because of his wisdom, many Christians would journey to seek his counsel and help. St. Athanasius (296AD-373AD) was a contemporary of St. Anthony and wrote a splendid book on his life.

Athanasius tells us that Anthony lived in solitude for two reasons. He wanted to increase his desire for Christ. Second, he wanted to have "fixity of purpose." Anthony wanted to develop a deep hunger and thirst for Christ in his own life and in the lives of those who came to see him. In addition, he wanted to be firm in his calling. He wanted others to have this "fixity of purpose," too.

Not all of us will be called by God to live a life of *total* solitude and silence. Some of us will. All of us, however, are called by God to have *some* solitude and silence so that we too develop a deep hunger and thirst for Christ and have that "fixity of purpose."

Remember the TV show called, *The Monastery*? It aired in May 2005. Five men entered the Benedictine monastery in Worth, UK, for forty days and forty nights. They went there to experience the silence and solitude of the monastery. Christopher Jamison is the Abbot of the monastery and he has now written a book entitled, *Finding Sanctuary: Monastic Steps for Everyday Life.* In it, he tells this story:

A Buddhist monk once said to me: 'The silence will teach you everything,' and this parallels a story of the desert fathers: 'A certain brother came to the abbot Moses seeking a word from him. And the old man said to him: "Go and sit in your cell, and your cell will teach you everything."' The ability to sit still, in silence, with nothing else except the silence really does frighten many people, and rightly so. Anthony of Egypt explains why: 'The one who sits in solitude and quiet has escaped from three wars: hearing, speaking and seeing; yet against one thing shall he continually battle: that is, his own heart.' (p. 41)

So the silence is there for a purpose: to disclose and unravel my heart before Christ and before myself. "What are my thoughts and feelings?" "What is driving me?" "What are my motives?" "What are my deepest attitudes and dispositions?" In other words, "Who am I?"

The silence will teach me everything. It is in the silence that I will find my true self. It is in the silence that I will discover Christ. It only takes a few minutes each day. The choice is mine.